Grow, Glow and Go!

31 Days of Devotions for Your Everyday Crazy

DeEsta Dawn Beets

www.DeEstaDawn.com

Sue,

I pray that God uses His Word + the short stories in this devotional to lift your spirits as you recover from your surgery and to give you the encouragement to keep pressing on to the adventures God has in store for you.

Love,
Desta Dawn

ACKNOWLEDGEMENTS

I first want to recognize my Lord and Savior, without Him I would have no purpose.

There are so many people that helped make this book come to life. I want to thank God for using my sister-in-Christ, Jerry, for telling me I ought to write a book. I want to continue by thanking my awesome crew of 5 who put up with me in our group texts every time I wanted their opinion on something and for their constant encouragement. Mom, Cati, Bam, Alli, & Tanner, you guys are true rocks in my life. Next I want to really let my pastor, Bro. John, know how much it meant to me for him to read my book and check the verses that I lined out each day. I am blessed to worship with this man that truly has a heart for God and only preaches the Truth. This book would also not be possible without the following individuals: Crystal Sparks for her mentoring skills that gave me the courage to dream big and Katherine Hartvickson for her coaching skills that helped me find my true calling and to Kay, Martha, and Ann for being a few of my first readers to give me honest feedback.

I also want to give an extra great big shout-out to my mom, Priscillia Greene, aka Miss Pris. Without her constant support and help editing this book, it would probably be in shambles. Words cannot express how important my mom is in my life and how much I love her. Now it's time for her to get her book completed so the world can see her amazing talent.

Finally, a big thank you… to you… my reader. I appreciate you picking this book up and giving it a whirl and pray it will bless you.

CONTENTS

Intro   The Beginning

Day 1   Stand Firm

Day 2   Supplies

Day 3   Running from the Enemy

Day 4   Sponge

Day 5   Sneak Attack

Day 6   Need Protection

Day 7   Negative Mindset

Day 8   A God's Eye View

Day 9   Wilting or Watering

Day 10   Start

Day 11   Clarity

Day 12   Dirty Dishes

Day 13   Shoes

Day 14   Disqualified

Day 15   Sandpaper

Day 16   Perishing

Day 17   Not as it Appears

Day 18   Dumpster Diver

Day 19   Famous

Day 20   "Those" People

Day 21   Vulnerable Yet Guarded

Day 22   Average

Day 23   Lifeline

Day 24   Chicken Poop

Day 25   Days vs Moments

Day 26   Cuts

Day 27   Patience

Day 28   I Screwed Up

Day 29   Sunglasses

Day 30   Gift Exchange

Day 31   Let's Grow, Glow & Go!!!

The End   Adventure Awaits You

Intro

THE
BEGINNING

....

Truly I thank you for picking up this book today. I hope the light of the Lord just explodes
from these pages. I've had a desire to write for
many years, but always the devil tries to wea-
sel his way in the crevices of my brain telling
me how inadequate I am. Problem is, that is
the furthest from the **TRUTH**. The only way to
know the Truth is to read it firsthand in God's
special handbook, scripted just for you and
me. As you go through each devotion that this
book contains, please have your Bible handy
and let the Spirit move you to keep reading
beyond the passages that I have lined out each
day. On your journey through this book, I
want to dwell on you seeing through the enemy lies and really looking in God's mirror of
how and who **He** designed you to be and who
He wants you to become. When there are days

you don't want to pick up this book, please please pick up **THE BOOK**, His Word and hold it dear and near to your heart. His Book is the **ONLY** book you will ever need in this lifetime. Picking up His Word is one simple step of obedience in a forward direction and one step further from your ever-present enemy, Satan.

I would love to hear from all of my readers. I want to see how God's Word is transforming you. Remember, change is not an overnight event; it is an everyday marathon and the road will get bumpy at times but hang tight and be strong and be courageous. You've got this!

Philippians 4:13, "I can do all things through Christ who strengthens me." (NKJV)

God Bless,
DeEsta

Just food for thought as you are reading throughout this book, any time I refer to the Devil or Satan, in many and in most circumstances in all actuality, it is the Devil's demons that are doing his bidding, not Satan himself. Always keep in mind that only God himself is omnipresent. Satan can **ONLY** be in one place at one time. He is not everywhere at all times as our Heavenly Father is with us. God can be with me in Texas and with you in Australia…at the exact same moment. Scripture backs this up in the following verses:

Proverbs 15:3 "The eyes of the Lord are everywhere, keeping watch on the wicked and the good." (NIV)

Psalms 139:3 "You discern my going out and my lying down; you are familiar with all my ways." (NIV)

Job 34:21 "For His eyes are on the ways of men, And he sees their every step." (NIV)

Jeremiah 23:24 "Can a man hide himself in secret places so that I cannot see him declares the Lord. Do I not fill heaven and earth? declares the Lord." (ESV)

Day 1

STAND FIRM

Before we begin…did you skip the Intro to this book? If you did, please go back and take a few minutes to read it. I wrote it just for you.

Now on to Day One's devotion.

Are you standing firm on your foundation? It is harder said than done, I readily admit. However, it is **NOT** impossible. The Devil will advance at us from every angle, every corner and in every season of our lives. We must stand firm no matter our circumstances. We can and **will** defeat our enemy **with** God Almighty backing us up.

I used to live in a neighborhood with the most awesome neighbors; however, one of my next-door neighbors had a vicious ankle biting Chihuahua. He only weighed in at about 8 pounds, but he might as well have been about 150 pounds! So… this one beautiful evening my husband and I were out visiting with them when suddenly, the little hellion comes barging out the side door and his mission was to annihilate anything in his path. And guess who he spotted first...yep... ME!!!! He had already bitten me once before only a few short months back, so I am speculating that the taste of my blood was blue-ribbon worthy, and he wanted another ribbon for the wall. But me being a girl who likes to have her blood well contained within the boundaries of my skin, my brain and body proceeded straight to PANIC mode! I began to retreat as fast as I could, all the while I was screaming for the creature to stand down. But to no avail, he kept advancing towards my precious frame and all I could imagine were his fangs ripping into my tender pale flesh!!!! But in a moment's notice, my husband, aka knight in shining armor, came to my rescue and jumped in between me and the ferocious beast. My husband stood his ground and the beast turned to putty. Yes, he barked a bit, but he lost his fight and bite and his focus was no longer on me. My husband later explained to me that if I had stood my ground, then the dog would know I wasn't cowering down and the miniature beast would have reconsidered his position.

This is EXACTLY what the enemy does to us. We must be wise to his schemes! He is out to bark, bite and make us retreat. God is our defender and He **will** intercede for us and **will** have our back **EVERY** time, AND... hear this... once saved... God has equipped us with **EVERYTHING** we need to defeat Satan. We just need to stand firm. Also, know that even though we are equipped, **God never wants us to stop turning to Him.**

Arm yourself and get ready to stand your ground, no retreating today! God and a legion of angels are out there backing us up when things get a little icky.

Luke 4:10 "For it is written: 'He will command His angels concerning you to guard you carefully; they will lift you up in their hands, so that you will not strike your foot against a stone.'" (NIV)

Psalm 34:7 "The angel of the Lord encamps around those who fear him, and he delivers them." (NIV)

Day 2

SUPPLIES

....

What supplies are you packing? And no, I'm not talking about your lipstick, ladies, or your wallet, gentlemen. I'm talking about what supplies have been purchased for you by God that you are not utilizing?

God gives us supplies such as grace, opportunities, choice, power, strength, confidence.

Hebrews 10:35 "So, don't lose your bold, courageous faith, for you are destined for a great reward!" (TPT).

Our Almighty calls us to do courageous feats on this earthly sphere. And when He calls **YOU** (yes, you) to conquer mountains larger than you have ever seen... by golly, you better know He has already given you the resources to tackle that Mt. Everest.

So what are you waiting for?

_____

_____

_____

Yes, I truly want you to list your excuse(s) above. Once you see it written, it will either seem little, insignificant, silly or an eye opener on where you need to ask God for some confidence and direction.

The last two books that I have read have been on seeking clarity for my life. These readings have been a wealth of information. Just one word has sparked an area that I deeply need to reflect on for a bit and dig deep, no matter how dirty it's going to get. I challenge you to do the same. Where is God wanting you to move and are you using the supplies He has already provided you?

So… Let's go tackle what God has given us. **Pray to God** for some direction and some clarity on the strengths He has given you this season, to tackle that monster that seems nearly impossible to slay. You **HAVE** got this. I believe in you. I believe in me. Sometimes we need to remind ourselves that we believe in ourselves.

How can we be encouragers to others, if we can't even believe in ourselves? Again...I can't repeat this enough...DO NOT listen to the enemy's lies!!!!! Liar, Liar, Pants on Fire!!!!! That about sums up our enemy. Plug your ears like a two-year old and walk away like a boss!

Reflect below on where God has been showing you areas to tackle where you have been hesitant.

_____

_____

_____

Discover the different spiritual gifts God gives in the following scriptures.

Romans 12:6-8
1 Corinthians 12:8-10
1 Peter 4:11

Now look at the scriptures about Fruits of the Spirit in **Galatians chapter 5**.

RUNNING FROM THE ENEMY

Are you tired of running? What are you running from? Take a moment before we go one step further, jot down who or what is keeping you hitting the pavement, panting, sweating and out of breath. What is leaving you with a chaotic spirit? Is it possibly past hurts that have torn you, or is it past hurts you have done to others? Is it the lies you tell yourself? What keeps you tense and cramped up in your sprint to escape?

_____

_____

_____

Once we have the spirit of Jesus residing in our hearts, we are no longer on the run from the enemy. We get to turn around, face our enemy and **demand** him to stop the ever-present torture of our heart and mind. He no longer holds the power of dictating our future. **Jesus Christ gets the privilege of loving us and shaping us and nurturing us.**

Isaiah 64:8 "But now, O Lord, You are our Father, we are the clay, and You our potter; and we all are the work of Your hand." (NKJV)

Stop right now, bow your head and ask Jesus to show you what you are running from and ask Him to give you the courage, power, and authority that He gave to you on that day you accepted Jesus as your personal Savior. If you have never accepted Christ as your personal Savior, please go to Chapter 30 of this book to learn how you can accept this beautiful gift.

2 Timothy 1:7 "For God gave us a spirit not of fear but of power and love and self-control." (ESV)

I want to use this short story to illustrate my point:

My "sweet" now six-year-old Chihuahua will have innocents running! To clarify, technically, he is only sweet to about five family members and is a terror to everyone else who dares enter his 3-mile radius. Let me explain how he keeps innocents on the run. In our former home, we lived in a neighborhood that had many friends for my girls to play with on the weekends. We had an open-door policy, however, the girls in the neighborhood understood they needed to knock and not just barge in because that "sweet" dog of mine became like the enemy and had even been called the spawn of Satan. He is a vicious ankle biter and would chase you relentlessly.

So that was the background story…now on to the plot…

One day Lacy (name changed to protect the innocent) came to our house, she creeped open the door and boldly entered our home. I was relaxing in our recliner with my 3-1/2 pound angel peacefully resting on my lap as Lacy confidently walks in and says, "Look he's not even barking at me." Before she could barely release the word "me," my angel became a beast and tore after the child! Lacy barreled back towards the front door to escape the teeth that were inches away from chomping down on her precious soft ankles. To my horror I could not get out of the chair quick enough to grab the pooch before he proceeded to chase her out the door, through the front yard...the whole time Lacy is screaming at the top of her lungs, arms flailing in the air, the dog snarling behind her and me trailing behind yelling at my canine to cease fire! Lacy proceeded to run across the road (I did check to be sure no oncoming vehicles were present) and up the incline of the neighbor's driveway which lead to a dead end, specifically the closed garage door. Seconds before she careened into the door, she became a genius. I saw her begin to shed her jacket and then just steps away from her demise she spun around and cloaked my pooch with her jacket! **She became brave, courageous and she faced her enemy head on and won the battle!** This sent the monster scurrying away with his tail between his legs squealing all the way to his den.

This is the power we have over the enemy. We don't have to keep running. **We get to face him and defeat him.** Don't let the enemy of your past or present keep you on an endless treadmill into the future. Please open God's

Word and read the passages herein to help drive this point home.

Leviticus 26:6 "I will grant peace in the land, and you will lie down and no one will make you afraid. I will remove savage beasts from the land, and the sword will not pass through your country." (NIV)

Romans 16:20 "And the God of peace will swiftly pound Satan to a pulp under your feet! And the wonderful favor of our Lord Jesus will surround you." (TPT)

Colossians is a great chapter to read, so I have highlighted these verses below for further reading.

Colossians 1:13-14
Colossians 2:15

Day 4

SPONGE

....

Have you ever seen a real sponge, not the synthetic ones at the grocery store, but the real life (well used to be alive) sponge that comes from the ocean? If they are alive in their natural habitat, they are squishy and spongy. However, pull them out of their environment and they get hard, brittle and rough.

This is exactly what happens to us when we are spiritually dry. We dry up, we can get hard-hearted, brittle and rough. Once we get back to the living water and stay in the waterfall of God's glory, our hearts become as flesh again and we begin to have a heart filled with warmth.

And don't we all want to be around the live sponge filled with His grace and love? Think about it like this...

Have you ever gotten in a play fight in the kitchen where a wet rag or wet sponge has been thrown your way? Now go back to the real life sponge…being hit with it in its natural squishy state will playfully slap you and lighten your mood… however, take the dry rough dead sponge and chunk that… boy howdy… your victim probably is no longer ready to play but ready to fight. That dry sponge will cause damage and leave a mark.

As Christians we need to let every person we touch with our words to be those of life, love, grace and understanding… not words of harshness, contempt or ugliness.

Get drenched in the Word. It's the only way we can be assured that we even have a minuscule chance of shining the light of Jesus. How to do this? Well, just by diving into devotionals like this, you are showing your desire to grow closer to Jesus. But more importantly, open **HIS WORD** and don't look back; you'll never regret a moment in His arms.

Ezekiel 11: 19 "And I will give them one heart, and a new spirit I will put within them. I will remove the heart of stone from their flesh and give them a heart of flesh." (ESV)

Ezekiel 36:26 "And I will give you a new heart, and a new spirit I will put within you. And I will remove the heart of stone from your flesh and give you a heart of flesh." (ESV)

Jeremiah 31:33 "For this is the covenant that I will make with the house of Israel after those days, declares the LORD: I will put my law within them, and I will write it on their hearts. And I will be their God, and they shall be my people." (ESV)

Hebrews 8:10 "For this is the covenant that I will make with the house of Israel after those days, declares the Lord: I will put my laws into their minds, and write them on their hearts, and I will be their God, and they shall be my people." (ESV)

SNEAK ATTACK

Have you ever felt like the Devil planted a booby-trap? Well...he probably did, **everything good is from God** and everything bad is from the enemy. Remember that when you think the Lord has tempted you or given you a punishment. It's NOT God! This is the enemy!!!! Satan knows how to push your buttons, trip you up, and how to destroy your testimony, marriage, friendships, businesses and the list goes on and on. Our Heavenly Father wants only the best for us; His Word clearly states it in **Matthew 7:11** "If you, then, though you are evil, know how to give good gifts to your children, how much more will your Father in heaven give good gifts to those who ask him!" (NIV)

I recently read a book and it really hits home, that our God does not strike us with disease or disaster...demons do. The enemy wants us to turn our back on Jesus and miss out on our rich blessings that have been bestowed upon us. The only way to be prepared for enemy attacks is to **ALWAYS** be on guard. The Devil doesn't take a day off, so neither can we.

Where is the enemy striking you in your life right this minute?

_____

_____

_____

It's okay to write it down; it's okay to speak it out loud. Let Satan know you know where he is hitting. Then louder than the words on this paper, start proclaiming out loud in Jesus' name the victory and start declaring scripture over your circumstances. Not sure where to find the exact verse... do an Internet search! And then pull out your trusty paper or hard back Bible and look it up as proof, don't even take Google for face value. **Know this, there is power in the Word!!!!!** Speaking it out loud makes our enemy tremble because he knows we are on to him.

Short Story:

I often feel like I have a zoo at my house on most days. I had been married to my husband for 5-1/2 years when this incident transpired. When we joined our families, he introduced me to the three most adorable kiddos, and I introduced him to the two most awesome boogersnots. All our children are not always with us at the same time, but when they are… along with three dogs and a cat, life can feel like a zoo, no question about it!

Well…

This one day when my precious (crazier than me, might I add) mother came to stay with us one night, she learned fairly quickly how we were training our pets to stay off our newly purchased furniture. I got this bright idea of purchasing a dog training mat online. This plastic device rolls out and covers your couch and when turned on, creates some static electricity. For all you dog lovers, don't worry, I did test it out personally for safety issues and to be sure my pets would not be harmed. It feels like static electricity, NOT a full-on shock, unless of course you lay or sit on it, but once a dog puts his or her paws on it, they immediately get off and realize this is the no-way zone.

So back to the story...

I had fully warned my beautiful, crazier than me mother, to be cautious of this as we were in training mode. All was good and dandy until the following morning when she FORGOT about the mat and decided to sit on it with only a thin layer of clothing covering her backside. Needless to say, she skyrocketed off the couch, bellowing unmentionables loud enough for possibly people in the next state to hear! I got a great laugh out of this... her... not so much!

I had my mom read this book prior to publishing and here is what she had to say about this said incident... "Let's just be clear here! It DOES NOT feel like static electricity! It feels like the Devil has strapped you in on Hell's couch & turned up the juice, then challenges you to break free without spewing uncontrollable words that you'll surely be sorry for!"

A couple of years have passed since this incident and she can now chuckle, however, I do sense a little tension with the chuckle!

This story just ties in that the enemy will plant sneak attacks. The Bible warns us, just like I had warned my mom, but we **always must be on guard.**

Please dig deeper in His Word of the Truth that is presented to us regarding today's lesson.

Ephesians 6:11 "Put on the whole armor of God, that you may be able to stand against the schemes of the devil." (ESV)

Revelation 12:11 "They conquered him completely through the blood of the Lamb and the powerful word of his testimony. They triumphed because they did not love and cling to their own lives, even when faced with death." (TPT)

Just for fun, I am throwing in the actual Facebook post my mom posted about today's story on her timeline on the day of the event.

Mom's Facebook post: "The rest of the story is... I spent the night at darling daughter's house so we could get up early so I could get an EGD procedure (like an endoscopy++). So, I'm half asleep & sit down on the couch... I didn't look back at the couch before I sat on it... who does that! Then I felt this electrical tingling sensation that sent me straight towards the ceiling with a VERY VERY BAD WORD! All the dogs and cats came to see what was the matter, along with my darling daughter!! Turns out she had placed the mat on the couch to teach the pets to stay off of it. Trust me, it'll work if they get on it even once... because I can tell you I'll never sit on the couch again!! LOL"

NEED PROTECTION?

Many of us were raised, as we should have been, to be independent, confident and self-sufficient. However, you must pause to realize that we cannot be all those things without God. He wants us to think, choose and do for ourselves...but... He wants us to do it through Him and to come to Him on **EVERYTHING** for guidance, companionship, knowledge and protection. We cannot do this alone or even with man's help. Let me repeat that... no matter how strong you are, or smart you are, or how long you have done it "on your own" ... you can **NOT** do this thing called life alone. You need God's protection along the way. And as crazy as it sounds, He will protect us every step of the way and He has even commanded angels to keep watch over us. How's that for having an ever-present bodyguard? I'm kinda diggin' it! Who said you had to be a movie star or the President to get your own bodyguard staff?

Matthew 26:53 "Don't you realize that I could ask my heavenly Father for angels to come at any time to deliver me? And instantly he would answer me by sending twelve armies of the angelic host to come and protect us." (TPT)

My mom raised me to be very independent and often that comes with me being a little opinionated and stubborn. Ummm, sometimes very stubborn. I think I can do anything, and I can take care of myself, thank you very much. But the truth be known. I'm a 5'5", 120-pound woman that realistically needs the help of others to accomplish so many things. And to prove this fact... even my dog thinks I need a little added protection.

Another dog story (When you have a zoo, it's easy to collect stories):

I have a beautiful 45-pound rescue dog named Michonne. She's a mix of Rottweiler, lab and terrier. She's great and she's also a big pain in the rear end. She's been to training classes and graduated from each class. According to

Michonne's trainer or maybe I should say, my trainer since I think I am being trained, Michonne is a very smart dog. She is also a very protective dog of me. I thought this was pretty awesome, and even warn people that when she is near me, they are not allowed to approach me. If we want to introduce her to any outsiders, my husband or our children must do the introduction. If I do it, she will show teeth and give warning signs for the approaching individual to back away. I thought this was an incredible trait and was honored that she was protecting me... however... come to find out she's only doing it 'cause she thinks I need the protection. And again, truth be told, if I was in a situation of an enemy attack, I would need her help and I would graciously accept it. Michonne becomes my protector because she knows that if the time comes, I will need assistance and she has my back.

Now, let's think about our Heavenly Father. He is so much bigger than a guard dog, so much bigger than a bodyguard, and so much bigger than you (no matter how big and bad you think you are). And He **NEVER** leaves your side!

Turn to **Deuteronomy 31:8** "It is the Lord who goes before you. He will be with you; He will not leave you or forsake you. Do not fear or be dismayed." (ESV)

We should be grateful that we don't have to look over our shoulder. You and I must always be aware, but never fear because our God and His army is constantly providing us His protection.

Question for you to ponder today. What keeps you from totally trust-falling into your Savior's arms today?

_____

_____

_____

Joshua 1:9 "Have I not commanded you? Be strong and courageous. Do not be frightened, and do not be dismayed, for the Lord your God is with you wherever you go." (ESV)

NEGATIVE MIND SET

....

Where do your let you mind go?

_____

_____

_____

Naturally, in this world our thoughts will gravitate to the negative side. Why is that? Why do we automatically gravitate towards the dark side?

_____

_____

_____

First, I believe it's because we live in a sinful world. Secondly, it's easier to throw a pity party because we are in a fallen world. Lastly, we can sometimes get more people on board to help throw that pity party and encourage us on the road that is destined for disaster. You might have come up with more examples; our excuses are probably endless.

Once we are constantly in a thorny and over-grown path, it's hard to see the beautiful blooming shrubs on the clear path lined with butterflies only a short jaunt away. When we stay on this path, we soon find that we will be caught by thorns and blood will flow. We will trip over vines and skin our knees. In order for us to change our thoughts, we must pull out sheers, loppers and a machete to clear the de-structive path and start putting one foot in front of the other one. One step at a time to get to the smooth, beautiful path that is just be-yond the bend.

Personal story:

So here is a tidbit of my personal experience:
Up until a couple of years ago, I didn't have much faith in man. And not just the human race, but the male species specifically. My track record wasn't playing out to how I thought it should. I saw that men were deserting and hurting me in my life, yet I desperately needed and wanted them to be a part of my journey.

Here are the examples that kept haunting my emotions. My biological father was absent most of my life and still is to this day. My stepdad left, my ex-husband left me, my grandfather passed away, my uncle passed away, my surgeon who operated on me six times, retired, and then my adoptive dad passed away. I just felt like, really? What other man wants to get up and leave? And I get that some of those relationships had no choice in the matter, death is inevitable. But this did not change my outlook that all these men were gone and out of my life.

But then a few years ago my thoughts changed; my heart changed, and this was due to searching for the Truth in the Word.

HELLO to DeEsta!!!! Let's think about the men that haven't left you… Your husband of 6+ years, your sons, your pastor and deacons, but most importantly… my Father and I'm not talking about the earthly one; I'm referring to God Almighty Himself and His son Jesus Christ. What more do I need if I have God and His Son? …No one… Absolutely… No one. And neither do you. Dear friends, we must wake up and see our victories! They outweigh the losses times infinity.

This revelation was life-altering to me. I had placed this huge value on men in my life and not value on the Creator Himself. Man will disappoint. Did you hear me? Man **WILL disappoint you.** However, **God will NEVER disappoint!** Remember, you are not perfect either and I am sure you have done plenty of disappointing yourself. Be careful not to be the pot that calls the kettle black if you can't even look in the mirror yourself.

Homework: Get in your brain, mind and heart. Start changing the negative ions to positive ions. You cannot change your environment, but you can change you.

Psalm 73: 23-26 "Nevertheless, I am continually with you; you hold my right hand. You guided with your counsel, and afterward you will receive me to glory. Whom have I in Heaven but you? And there is nothing on earth that I desire besides you. My flesh and my heart may fail, but God is the strength of my heart and my portion forever." (ESV)

Day 8

A GOD'S
EYE VIEW

One Saturday morning as I was sitting outside at my former home, I was just truly amazed at how mighty and tall the big oak trees were in my back yard. They just towered above me and I saw birds, wasps, and locusts within their branches. Then my eyes drifted downwards to my average size, fenced-in backyard and thought... yuck! When I first moved into that house, our backyard was overgrown with bamboo that was ever encroaching on our back doorstep. So, I had purchased poison to kill the bamboo, but that also meant I was killing off all the grass. So, my yard looked sickly, yes there was grass in sporadic places, but to say the least, my backyard was severely lacking in eye appeal... unless you looked at it as God's creation and through a God's eye view.

God's eye doesn't just see what's at face value. He sees what can't be seen with eyes alone.

What I saw: Dirt.

What He sees: Grass just below the dirt's surface, ready to burst through into dawn's new light.

What I saw: Gopher trails... aka... stupid mounds of dirt that make more trails than the lines on a road map, and I might add, ground that is now worthy of ankle twisting.

What He sees: A gopher and his family that has made their home securely beneath the ground's surface.

What I saw: Bugs worthy of squashing.

What He sees: Bugs scurrying around helping to cultivate the land and helping complete the cycle of life.

What I saw: Nothing more than a desolate yard in serious need of a landscaper.

What He sees: Past footprints of His creation that once tread here hundreds or thousands of years ago.

It's time we start realizing that life is so valuable, precious and so rich just beneath the surface and we need to grasp it through a God's eye view, not our own. We tend to only see the surface of ourselves and others, but not really grabbing what's underneath, and not realizing what God is seeing just beneath the surface. He sees all the goodness and knows just when we are in those desolate times. He knows that there are strong roots just below the surface ready to sprout out and create something new. However, **we must dig deep**, but this only comes **through the Word of God** and **hearing His voice** every step of the way. He will show you what lies beneath, and you need to know that it is good, very good.

Genesis 1:27 "So God created mankind in his own image, in the image of God he created them; male and female he created them. (NIV)

Genesis 1:31 "God saw all that he had made, and it was very good." (NIV)

Time for reflecting... This is always a difficult issue for most of us...but... where do you find yourself lacking and need to do a good eye flushing and start seeing you and others through a God's eye view?

_____

_____

_____

Day 9

WILTING OR WATERING?

....

Have you ever seen a Peace Lily? They typically remind me of a funeral plant, since I see one at every funeral I have ever attended. What I love about this plant is that it is easy to read. What I mean by this is you know when it needs watering and some TLC. The tell-tale sign that this plant needs water is the droopy leaves. These leaves will sink down so much that the leaves will drag the ground.

This is exactly what happens in our spiritual life. If we don't water ourselves with God's Word and His everlasting love, we begin to wilt. We don't always notice the results, but it is for sure that those around us will read us and they can see the effect of us getting God's steady stream of water.

Back to the Peace Lily, once you water it, within a couple of hours its leaves will begin to spruce up and will look fresh and healthy in no time. The same is true, once we get soaked in God's Word and His embrace, we will radiate healthy again and in no time at all. God patiently waits for our return. He just needs us to come to Him so He can water us with all His provisions. He does this freely.

So why is it we step out of His daily dose of amazing? I think most of the time we let the stresses of this world get in our way. We stop turning to God first; we give up. Don't misunderstand me. We will not always have a 100% perfect day every day even if we are totally lined up to God's constant shower. We will have troubles; Jesus clearly states that fact. But let me just remind you, the struggle is manageable as long as you **stay in His waterfall of goodness.**

Isaiah 44:3 "For I will pour water on the thirsty land, and streams on the dry ground; I will pour out my Spirit on your offspring, and my blessing on your descendants." (NIV)

Isaiah 58:11 "The Lord will guide you always; he will satisfy your needs in a sun-scorched land and will strengthen your frame. You will be like a well-watered garden, like a spring whose waters never fail." (NIV)

Psalm 63:1 "O God of my life, I'm lovesick for you in this weary wilderness. I thirst with the deepest longings to love you more, with cravings in my heart that can't be described. Such yearning grips my soul for you, my God!" (TPT)

How often are you opening God's word?

_____

_____

_____

How often are you allowing God to water your spirit?

_____

_____

_____

START

••

Start.

Just Start.

Start Today.

Start.

Yes. Start. Right. Now.

Start this Instant.

I'm sorry… are you still waiting? I said…

START!

This was my word for 2019. Even with my exponential growth with my GROW word for 2018, I have always been the girl who will START on Monday or START tomorrow or START on January 1st. Heeeeey you guys!!!! … Don't wait another millisecond. **START!**

Why do we do that? Why wait till tomorrow? Next week? Next year? Quit letting the devil talk you into delaying your blessings for another moment. God wants us to enjoy His riches NOW! We can't do that unless we **START!** and **START NOW!**

Take a moment… What are you waiting to START?

_____

_____

_____

Now, let's go pull out some biblical principle of God wanting us to start and not stand still, however, there is a season for standing still too.

Let me encourage you to START today and do it for 21 days. They say it takes 21 days to create a habit, but only one day to fall out of a habit. Once you START, do. not. stop!

Luke 11:9-10 "So I say to you, ask, and it will be given to you; seek, and you will find; knock, and it will be opened to you. For everyone who asks receives, and he who seeks finds, and to him who knocks it will be opened." (NKJV)

James 1:22-25 "But be doers of the word, and not hearers only, deceiving yourselves. For if anyone is a hearer of the word and not a doer, he is like a man observing his natural face in a mirror; for he observes himself, goes away, and immediately forgets what kind of man he was. But he who looks into the perfect law of liberty and continues in it, and is not a forgetful hearer but a doer of the work, this one will be blessed in what he does." (NKJV)

CLARITY

· ·

What is your word for this year? _____

Did you choose a word for this year? Well, up until 2018, neither did I. At first learning of this, I thought it rather odd. But think about it... God gave us a book that is filled with words to teach us and mold us. Words are powerful and if used the correct way, can pave the way for success in every aspect of our lives.

Clarity is not the word I choose as my bill-board word, but this in fact is a great word. Do you have clarity about where you are? Do you have clarity about where you are going? Do you have clarity about where you have been? You need to get a grasp on all three of those questions in order to grow.

Imagine you get in your car and there are a few bird poop piles on your windshield. You think nothing of this mess... until... a raindrop splatters on the glass in front of you. Before you think about the lonely few drops of rain that has plopped on the tempered glass... you click the windshield wipers on... this in turn streaks the poop piles to a white sloppy mess across your windshield which, in turn, shields you from seeing the danger that lurks on the outside. Without clarity of where you are going, you are bound to careen into your demise. So, what are you going to do? Well, hopefully you have wiper fluid and you are going to spray that bad boy like crazy and try to clean up the mess to get a clear view ahead.

This same scenario works in our lives. We can have such a mess right in front of us, but we don't notice it until it's too late. At that point we need to douse ourselves in God's living water and wash all that mess out and stand fresh and anew in His presence. What would be even better yet is to NEVER leave His embrace.

Romans 12:1-2 "I appeal to you therefore, brothers, by the mercies of God, to present your bodies as a living sacrifice, holy and acceptable to God, which is your spiritual worship. Do not be conformed to this world, but be transformed by the renewal of your mind, that by testing you may discern what is the will of God, what is good and acceptable and perfect." (ESV)

I encourage you to choose a word every year to be your focus of what you want in and for your life. My first word for 2018 was GROW. I loved this word and I kept it close to mind every day. Guess what? That year I grew leaps and bounds. It was exciting, but it took a lot of hard work. The next year I had trouble choosing a word... but God always comes through and he will speak to you. My word just came to me out of nowhere and I knew it was God speaking to my heart.

Tomorrow I will tell you what my word was for 2019.

Day 12

DIRTY DISHES

Children can be a 'cough' 'cough'…um…shall I say challenge on some days. But hey I'm always up for a good challenge. So, here's my story…

I gave a chore to one of my I-do children to accomplish while I was at work. Once I arrived home, I expected to find the chore completed to my satisfaction. I instead found it half done and not done correctly. This child's name has been changed to protect the guilty. Let's call him Andrew. Andrew had already left to go back to his mom's house, and I would not be seeing him for several days. This meant that after an exhausting day at work, I had to re-do his chore that consisted of me unloading the dishwasher and starting Andrew's chore all over again.

This process really got me to thinking…how many times do we do a job halfway because no one was there to see? However, our Heavenly Father is always watching and wants us to give it our all when no one is around to supervise or to sing our praises.

What have you been slacking on?

_____

_____

_____

What can you improve on today?

_____

_____

_____

Go out there and make it great, even if it is just doing the dishes!

1 Corinthians 10:31 "So whether you eat or drink, or whatever you do, do it all for the glory of God." (NIV)

Day 13

SHOES

Shoes are a girl's best friend. Well... at least a lot of women I know love to go shoe shopping. I, on the other hand, don't particularly care for shoe shopping... unless it is for a pair of UGGs or a comfortable pair of tennis shoes.

What shoes are you wearing? Are you trying to be someone you are not? Are you trying to appease man and have forgotten to look towards God? If God gifted you with a high-heel style, rock it like it's nobody's business. But if God has gifted you with steel-toe boots to go out and get tough and rough, you better toss those heels like a blaze has just ignited the strap!

God designed us perfectly even though we are the ever-imperfect mess. He wants us to use the gifts and talents He has assigned specifically to us, not what He has given your spouse, friend, boss, or parent. Stop trying to be them and **BE YOU!!!!** You will begin excelling to levels you never knew were in the game once you gain insight on this. Get comfortable in the shoes God designed for your feet on your personal path.

Proverbs 3:6 "In all your ways submit to him, and he will make your paths straight." (NIV)

I own my own business. My gift is not the financial side. Yes, I do some of it because I am a small business owner, but this is NOT my gift or my passion. Because of this I have hired someone who is qualified in this area to help me and teach me, but I rely on them to handle the bulk of it. I am, however, excellent with customer service. I enjoy people. I love people. I am social. This is where I love to be, with the people, and this is what I cultivate in my business. However, there are still other roles required, such as sales; but I still get to look at that as interaction with people and like I said, I love people!

Something else I have learned, is people love you most when you are you. So who are you? Yes, I want you to actually jot down some thoughts below. Then start exploring who you are and the God-given designer shoes He has provided you.

_____

_____

_____

Proverbs 3:5 "Trust in the Lord with all your heart and lean not on your own understanding." (NIV)

Day 14

DISQUALIFIED

∙∙∙

You ARE beautifully and wonderfully made. **Proverbs 31:25** states "Strength and honor are her clothing; She shall rejoice in time to come." (NKJV). On this planet we will have our families, friends, colleagues, social media, news, and magazines tell us we are not qualified to write a book, sing a song, be a parent, travel the world, run a company, go into ministry, etc. But is that the truth? If you just said, "No", that's great but do you really believe that deep down? If you said, "Yes," then friend we need to have a little chat. If we are getting disqualifications from those around us, keep remembering that the Devil is a LIAR!!!!! And his punk self is using people and things around you to LIE to YOU! **STOP** believing it!

Short story:

Many years ago, my dad and I used to do sales calls together at my business. I'll never forget this one sales presentation we did at a furniture store in the neighboring town. We sat down with the proprietor and were telling him all the details of what opening an account with our company would look like for his business. Every time the owner asked a question, my dad would look to me to answer as he was training me to be the best sales rep. Each and every time this happened, the owner would IGNORE me and again direct his questions to my dad. To say the least it was infuriating. This man was trying to disqualify my knowledge, my position, and my humanity... well at least my authority as a woman. We did close the deal that day but every time that client called our office, he NEVER asked to speak with me. He again was trying to disqualify what I had been qualified to do.

When God qualifies you for something... don't let anyone or anything try to take that away from you. That is the enemy trying to steal what God has assigned for only you.

2 Corinthians 3:5 "Yet we don't see ourselves as capable enough to do anything in our own strength, for our true competence flows from God's empowering presence." (TPT)

SANDPAPER

Jesus held so many different titles: physician, teacher, son. But today we are going to consider his carpentry skills. As I began this particular devotion, I decided to Google what an ancient sandpaper might have consisted of, which I thought might have been a pumice stone; but upon more research here is what I learned. In the original Greek translation, it states that Joseph, Jesus' father was a tekton, not necessarily a carpenter. Tekton is defined as a craftsman including a builder, carpenter, masonry or stonemason. According to my research, it presumes that given the time period and location of where Mary, Joseph and Jesus lived, it was more likely he was a stonemason. Regardless of the type of tekton skills they had, whether being wood or stone, I believe I can still relate my analogy of the sandpaper. I believe whether you are working with wood or stone, you will have to sand to make a fine finish.

Thanks for staying with me on this. I was excited to learn something new and thought it very valuable to share it with you in today's lesson. It's like we envision Eve eating an apple, but it has always been the forbidden fruit. We don't know the exact type of fruit. And what about Jonah and the whale? We don't know if it was a whale; the Bible says large fish. For all we know it was the biggest catfish ever seen in Texas! They say it's all bigger in Texas. Okay back to the basis of today's lesson.

I know a little bit about woodworking and am not afraid to let the sawdust fly. But in the 21st century most of my tools are electric. I've often considered what Jesus had to work with during His time. I seriously can't imagine using a hand saw on EVERY cut and getting the cut the EXACT dimension desired. Being off on your cut even by a 1/16th of an inch can throw your whole project out of whack. On top of that, it must have been a painstakingly difficult job in sanding down projects to get the beautiful finish.

Here is the thing, different grits get different jobs done. The rougher the project the tougher the grit. God is like that with us in different seasons of our life. Sometimes He must bring out the rough stuff to really work on your frayed edges. Keep in mind that this will happen throughout your life. You never get finished being roughed up. My point is, as you learn and grow and follow God's direction, He begins to put the finishing touches and begins to use a fine sandpaper to really get you smooth and to a polished finish.

It's hard to be roughed up, but the polished masterpiece in the end is well worth the grit.

Philippians 1:6 "And I am sure of this, that he who began a good work in you will bring it to completion at the day of Jesus Christ." (ESV)

Day 16

PERISHING

....

Proverbs 29:18
"When there is no clear prophetic vision, people quickly wander astray. But when you follow the revelation of the word, heaven's bless fills your soul." (TPT)

It's okay to dream and have visions for your future. Guess what? God's plans are a million times better than what we could ever imagine. He wants us to dream our dreams and go for them. Just always remember we want to stay in His will for our life, so start dreaming; this is one-way God speaks to us. However, you must **stay in the Word** and don't lose your lifeline with God, as you want to be sure you are following His designed plans for your life, not your own. We want to see His vision for our life.

Here is a vision I had for a room in my home:

When we bought our new house, I had this incredible vision of having my very own shabby chic room. It was for me to do my writings, crafts, reading and personal relaxation. I got on Pinterest and pinned all these fabulous pins of shabby chic ideas and the beautiful pieces I wanted to have in the room, but before long, I began to realize my shabby chic room turned into a very feminine vintage room. My vision did come to life and I got to have a room for writing, reading, relaxation and crafts; however, the details got changed a bit along the way. Have focus, don't lose sight, but remember that God can change the details along the way and that's okay.

Be open to His changes and direction for your life. There is so much more than we could possibly hope for just around the bend.

I want to encourage you to start a vision board and/or a dream book and start laying out your journey. I have both, and find them very instrumental in my focus; however, I don't become so laser focused that I forget to consult the One who knows where the roadblocks are up ahead. Don't be scared. No matter what stage of life you are in or what predicament you are in, **DREAM** and **VISUALIZE** what's just a step ahead.

Please take a moment to dream a little and see if you can visualize what might be in store for your future. Write down some things that popped in your head and perhaps some that you have long forgotten. Then pray about them and see what was just a whim and what was from God. Perhaps it's time to step outside our comfort zone.

My dreams and visions:

_____

_____

_____

_____

_____

_____

_____

_____

_____

_____

_____

_____

Now every day come back to these and see what you need to develop.

Day 17

NOT AS IT APPEARS

....

Did you know that the yellow dashes on the black asphalt of a highway are spaced 10 feet from one another? Unless you knew this answer, I bet you thought they were about 1-2 feet apart. When you are driving at a high rate of speed the appearance of the space makes them look closer together.

Things are not always as they appear...

Adam and Eve were in the garden and so very tempted by the beautiful fruit on the tree. Its outward appearance looked perfect for the taking, however, they were deceived by appearances and outside influence. See Genesis Chapter 3.

Things are not always as they appear...

For instance, a book. Better yet, let's look at **THE BOOK, HIS BOOK**. At first glance it appears to just be words, black, typed lettering on thin, white pages. However, if you open your heart, you find SO much more. It's an instruction manual; it's a medical directory; it's a story; it's a biography; it's motivational; it's a financial study; it's an adventure; but most importantly, it's a love story filled with love letters directly from God, straight to you AND it's a living source of life.

Appearances can be so deceiving. Don't see a book. See the greatest work ever written in all of eternity. Take time today to open God's Word and embark on a new discovery. Your eyes will see like never before, your heart will blaze a fire like you've never felt and your spirit will fly to heights unknown.

Not sure where to start in your new reading endeavor? Well, anywhere is a good "where" to start. But if you have never dived in and you are new in your walk with Jesus, might I suggest you start in the New Testament and perhaps even start in the Book of John.

John 1:6 "There was a man sent from God whose name was John." (NKJV)

DUMPSTER DIVER

••

I have this sweet adorable black and brown Chihuahua. She was given to us by some friends. She has spunk and is a little spontaneous with all her actions. Perhaps she has ADHD like me. But one thing I don't understand about her is her need to dumpster dive. Let me explain.

Leave this dog in any room with a garbage can and she will inevitably have it dumped over, or at the very least, have every shred of garbage pulled out to see if any goodies were left to waste.

Why does she do this? We feed her doggie treats and a decent brand of dog food. Why does she always go for the lesser of what she has been given? Perhaps we could ask ourselves this same question.

God generously provides **ALL** our needs, and more often than not, He also is providing so many of our wants. Yet here we are going to the garbage in the many things we do. Are you dumpster diving in smutty books, less than appropriate television, wrong friends, wrong relationships? This list can go on and on. God has already provided a path for you in great books (let's start with His), perfectly good shows and movies fit for a family, friends that have your back, and a spouse that is perfectly fit for you. We only need to wait on **HIS timing** and wait for **HIS gifts**. Quit opening the packages of the ugly and wait on His gifts. He's got the good stuff and it's way better than us dumpster diving. We are of His royal blood once we accept Jesus Christ as our personal savior. We no longer need to scavenge; **our Father provides** to us on a golden platter.

John 3:16 "For God so loved the world that He gave His only begotten Son, that whoever believes in Him should not perish but have everlasting life." (NKJV)

Romans 12:6-8 "Having then gifts differing according to the grace that is given to us, let us use them: if prophecy, let us prophecy in proportion to our faith; or ministry, let us use it in our ministering; he who teaches, in teaching; he who exhorts, in exhortation; he who gives, with liberality; he who leads, with diligence; he who shows mercy, with cheerfulness." (NKJV)

FAMOUS

....

Let's make Jesus famous.

Let's study His every move.

Let's use Him as our guide to life.

Here is the thing, a lot of us can tell everything about a famous actor or actress or perhaps even all the details on an infamous criminal. But we neglect the most important person, Jesus.

Why are we so drawn to the tabloids and the 5 o'clock news? I can tell you why. It's juicy gossip and it is way better than our lives ... in the way that we thank God that it is them and not us. Can I get an Amen? We get so caught up in others' lives we forget about the task at hand in our own and in that of our families. Again, this is where Satan is stealing from you. Don't let him take any more! Satan tries to divert your attention from Jesus every chance he gets, even when you are at the check-out line scoping out the gossip columns on display.

You know what, if you want gossip and drama and something better than TV, go straight to the Bible. There are stories of deception, murder, adultery, war, violence, love, intimacy and betrayal. It's all in there and it is oh so juicy. Let's get in the mindset that **Jesus has it all**, because that in fact is the **truth**.

Philippians 4:19 "And my God will supply every need of yours according to his riches in Glory in Christ Jesus." (ESV)

Let's make Jesus famous. Let's give Him the attention He deserves. Let's learn about Him, follow Him and trust Him. Let's strive to be like Him. Let's talk about Him daily in our families' lives and in our friends' lives. Plant seeds, water them and watch Jesus do His thing.

Know as I say this, when you are daily conversing about our Lord, don't be one of "THOSE" people. Don't be overbearing in your approach. I'll explain more in tomorrow's devotion. For now and always, JUST be loving.

Matthew 10:7 "And as you go, preach, saying, 'The kingdom of heaven is at hand.' " (NKJV)

2 Corinthians 5:20 "We are therefore Christ's ambassadors, as though God were making his appeal through us. We implore you on Christ's behalf: Be reconciled to God." (NIV)

Day 20

"THOSE" PEOPLE

....

Have you ever known one of "those" church people? The crazy, annoying human that thinks they know EVERYTHING about the Bible. For a minute, you think possibly they walked through all of time beginning with Adam and Eve. They think if you don't agree with one shred of their knowledge, then you are doomed to Hell. They think because you said a cuss word and they only speak in tongues, you are the scum of the Earth. Well…I have, and let me tell you something, "those" people are what turns ordinary people against what God has in store for them. I wish "those" people wouldn't act all holier-than-thou. Perhaps they need to go back and read, **Matthew 7:4** "Or how can you say to your brother, 'Let me remove the speck from your eye'; and look, a plank is in your own eye?" (NKJV) Perhaps they should read Jesus conversing with the lady at the well. Go visit **John 4** and the love Jesus showed the Samaritan woman. If you have ever known one of "those" people or perhaps maybe you are even one of "those" people, it's time to make some changes. Here is a fact, we are all sinners and fall short of the Glory of God **(Romans 3:23).** But because of Jesus' sacrifice, we get to live in His grace. God does not see you as better than me or Billy Graham better than Oprah. He sees our hearts and He wants us to live according to how Jesus lived. This is the reason that He sent Himself in human form, so you could see how it should be done.

Here's another thing...just because I sin differently than others, does not make them better, and we all need correction and direction, but we all need it given out of **LOVE**.

Don't let "those" people stop you from attending church...yea yea yea, I don't have to go to church, I can have church wherever I am because God is with me. I hear this sooooo much. This is very true my friend, however, He designed the church for you and me. We are the church and the church is a body of people coming together to worship the Lord and fellowship and get the camaraderie you can only get around other believers. Can "those" people be your sisters or brothers in Christ? Absolutely! Love them anyway. They are no better than you and you are no better than them. We all have our own demons to battle and the church is our hospital. Don't be a hypocrite and not attend church because there are hypocrites there. Guess what? There are hypocrites EVERYWHERE you go. Get over it and don't let the Devil rob you again of your joy and time to worship the Lord with other believers.

Take a moment to reflect to see if you are one of "those" people or if you are one that needs to show a little grace to "those" people. I have a feeling I have come across individuals at some point in my life as one of "those" people, and I am sorry for that, but I have been forgiven and grace has been extended. And it can and will be for you.

Please read the verse below and focus on the last 3 words...

1 Peter 3:15 "But in your hearts set apart Christ as lord. Always be prepared to give an answer to everyone who asks you to give the reason for the hope that you have. But do this with gentleness and respect." (NIV)

VULNERABLE YET GUARDED

Today we are going to do a little science experiment. I want you to get a balloon. Blow it up and tie the knot in it. Then I want you to get a small piece of scotch tape and place it anywhere on the balloon. Now go grab a pin or needle and insert the needle through the scotch tape.

What happened? If all went right, the balloon should not have popped. It will now leak air, but not explode. This is a cool science project. Don't ask me how it works, it just does and we will leave it at that; or if you are really curious, go search it on the web. By now can you tell I do A LOT of web searches?

I will compare us to this balloon science experiment. We are in a constant vulnerable position as humans. We come in to contact with the outside world second-by-second. The outside world, when we think of people, can be vicious. Talk about roaring lions...they are everywhere. Whether it be at your job, the grocery store, church, at a family gathering or perhaps in your own home with your spouse or children, people bite and OFTEN! We need to be vulnerable so we can feel compassion and love, but we also need to guard ourselves. God wants us to be aware of our surroundings and put up boundaries and protections so we don't let toxic people ruin us.

When we are well guarded, we won't pop or explode when we get pricked by someone's harsh words or tone of voice. We won't get hurt beyond repair when someone comes barking and biting at us.

Just like the tape is the guard for the balloon, we need to make the Bible our guard for our hearts.

Philippians 4:6-7 "Do not be anxious about anything, but in everything by prayer and supplication with thanksgiving let your requests be made known to God. And the peace of God, which surpasses all understanding, will guard your hearts and your minds in Christ Jesus." (ESV)

Matthew 7:6 "Do not give dogs what is holy, and do not throw your pearls before pigs, lest they trample them underfoot and turn to attack you." (ESV)

Day 22

AVERAGE

....

Average.

Average just sounds like an average word.

Do you want to be average?

Do you want to live an average life?

I know I don't. I want to be exceptional, amazing, smart, talented; the list goes on and on. And guess what? God wants us to be more than average. He wants us to always strive for more.

More connection with Him, more connection with others, more connection with yourself. He has gifted you with incredible gifts. So **START** using them. If you are not sure what gifts, think about what you are passionate about. Maybe cooking, hosting, or writing is your passion. No matter what it is, do it with everything you have.

Colossians 3:23 "Whatever you do, work at it with all your heart, as working for the Lord, not for men." (NIV)

Maybe you can't be a chef on television, at least not right now, but you can make the meanest enchiladas on the block. You can search great recipes on the web and watch You Tube videos on how the pros do it. You can get better and better and better.

Guess what I found out though…you can't get better by sitting in front of the television watching everyone else's dreams come true. (By the way this can also be the enemy pulling you away from God's calling for your life.) You need to get up and start living your best life now. Guess what, you can't wait till tomorrow, or Monday or January 1st. You need to **START** now.

Motivation is hard to find some days. I totally understand. Fighting to beat average is difficult. It seems like the more I fight being non-average, the more it tugs at me. There are some days that I have taken that television binge and then regretted what I could have accomplished. This is another reason I look at my vision board or dream book every day. You will not always have someone else around to hold yourself accountable, so you will need to find the inner strength to do this and rely on His strength to get you to heights you never thought possible.

Philippians 4:13 "I can do everything through him who gives me strength." (NIV)

LIFELINE

....

Remember the TV show, "Who Wants To Be a Millionaire?" If not, here is the rundown. This very popular television show selected a person to sit in a seat, center stage, and answer questions. Every time you answered a question correctly, your running total of money kept increasing. However, if you got stumped on a question, you could use one of three lifelines to help rescue and try to get you closer to that million dollars. Just so you know, the three lifelines were, call to a friend, 50/50 (they would remove half of the wrong answers) and ask the audience.

Well, Jesus is our lifeline and we don't need three choices. **He is the only way**; the only lifeline to eternal salvation. Jesus said in **John 14:6** "...I am the way and the truth and the life. No one comes to the Father except through Me." (NIV) If you are ready to accept Jesus Christ as your personal savior, please turn to Day 30's devotion. Like right now, before you finish reading this devotion. Once you have accepted Jesus as your Lord and Savior, He is your constant and steady lifeline.

You never see a ship head out to sea without ample lifelines for use if their ship or crew is in distress. This is the same for your life. Jesus always needs to be aboard your vessel and you never want to let too much slack in your lifeline, as Jesus must be close to you in order to help guide your path and keep you afloat.

Hebrews 13:5-6 "Let your conduct be without covetousness; be content with such things as you have. For He Himself has said, 'I will never leave you nor forsake you.' So we may boldly say: 'The Lord is my helper; I will not fear. What can man do to me?'" (NKJV)

CHICKEN POOP

My family and I recently got a chicken coup and ten beautiful chickens. Eight of them are Reds and two of them are Buff Laced Polish. I guess the older I get, the more I appreciate all this natural God-given beauty around me. Next, I am thinking about being a beekeeper. Oh, where was I? Back to my story. BEAUTY, external beauty to be exact, is where I want to go with this.

These chickens are beautiful! However, external beauty can be just an illusion, because you don't see their stinky poop. I mean I was shocked to see the amount of poop that one chicken can produce. I've had rabbits, fish, birds, cats, hamsters, guinea pigs, and all their poop seemed reasonable to the size of the creature. However, chicken poop is BIG, GROSS and it splatters a disgusting mess! And with all those chickens, it's a little smelly.

Well, us humans can be the same way. We can be freshly showered and shaven, have nicely pressed clothes, hair in impeccable order; yet we can have our innermost self stinking up the whole barn! When you are not living your life to His Word, then eventually your inside intentions, feelings, emotions and actions will start tainting the outside appearance.

Granted my chickens are still beautiful as they are God's creation, but I can see the mess, poo, and dirty tail feathers the more I am around them. We need to be constantly cleaning up the inside. Cleaning up our thoughts, emotions and intentions. Everything we do every day needs to begin to align with God's Word. Is this hard? You betcha it's hard. Are you going to go backwards sometimes? Absolutely! Keep moving forward anyway. If we turn back or give in, we are just letting the enemy get a foothold and we don't want to give him anything but a beating. We need to know we can do this. **START** thinking today! What can you **START** cleaning up to get you one step closer to God's design and purpose for your beautiful life?

_____

_____

_____

_____

Matthew 15:18 "...But what comes out of your mouth reveals the core of your heart..." (TPT)

DAYS VS MOMENTS

•••

Are you focused on the days or the moments? I was watching a movie called, "Christmas in Love" on the Hallmark Channel and the actress said, "It's not about the days, it's about the moments."

This hit me square in the gut. It spoke so loud and clear to me.

Sometimes we get so laser-focused and zeroed in on our destinations and the goal line that we forget to take in the moments that get us there. When we are truly trying to follow God's will for our life, we shouldn't try to time warp past the experiences God wants us to observe along the way. These are moments and we can use those moments as enjoyment and learning. This is one of God's blessings. Do NOT concentrate on the fact that it has taken you X amount of days or even years to reach that finish line. Think more about the journey and the moments along the way. This is preparing **you** for **your** future. Preparing **you** for the goal, dream, or vision that you are working towards. God wants you to be prepared and grateful for what you have achieved. Remember there are **no** short cuts.

Proverbs 16:3 "Commit to the Lord whatever you do and your plans will succeed." (NIV)

Day 26

CUTS

....

If you have ever been in the kitchen prepping meals, it's likely you have cut yourself with a knife or even possibly the grater.

There is a SHARP and immediate pain that is present as the blade pierces your skin and signals your nerves that got sliced to tell your brain to draw your hand back and FAST! It is our automatic reaction to pain - to RETREAT.

So where am I taking this? Taking you down a path to compare it to your relationships and the pain we can even feel from fellow Christian brothers and sisters. Have you ever had a wonderful church home and someone has cut you to the core? Well, if you have been in ANY church long enough, I'd be surprised if your answer was anything less than a resounding

YES! No matter if it was a fellow church member, friend, family or business associate; we will be hurt, and the pain will be felt. What we need to keep in mind is how can you take that pain and grow from it?

If you leave a wound unattended, it will fester with puss and infection. Not a pretty picture? Well, isn't that what will happen to you if you don't address the pain others have caused?

People are going to fail us, and we are going to fail people. Keep in mind there are seasons in which you mend fences and there are seasons where you lock up the gates at fences. We have boundaries that we need to keep guarded. But don't let past wounds keep you from loving again, from following your passion, from getting close to another friend or even from finding a new church home or staying at the one you are in at present.

One of the solutions to getting a wound healed is to see a doctor. Spiritually, Jesus is our doctor. His advice to us will be to **forgive**. That is such a dirty word to many people. But **for-giveness is such a beautiful and freeing word**. Forgiveness is not for the other person as much as it is for you.

Second, open your heart to someone. Jesus is the only Counselor we will ever need, however, even He understands we are only human, and He tells us it is okay for us to get guidance from wise individuals.

Proverbs 12:15 "The way of a fool is right in his own eyes, But he who heeds counsel is wise." (NKJV)

Proverbs 11:14 "Where there is no counsel, the people fall; But in the multitude of counselors there is safety." (NKJV)

I have seen counselors many times throughout my life. I have drawn encouragement from them. I have learned how to better face the unknown future. Whether it is a counselor, parent, sibling, pastor or friend, don't battle this alone.

What are you battling? I know there is something right now in your life that is festering, and you are ignoring it. Jesus cares and I can assure you there is someone in your life that cares too. Reach out and don't do this alone. Remember this time is but for a season.

2 Timothy 3:16-17 "Every scripture has been written by the Holy Spirit, the breath of God. It will empower you by its instruction and correction, giving you the strength to take the right direction and lead you deeper into the path of godliness. Then you will be God's servant, fully mature and perfectly prepared to fulfill any assignment God gives you." (TPT)

Day 27

PATIENCE

....

We always seem to try to take things in our own hands. When will we realize we are not always the best at leading the pack? In Exodus 32 Aaron, Moses' brother, got impatient. When things got sticky and Aaron was under fire with his peers, He crumbled. He and God's people got tired of waiting. We need to remember to wait on God's timing. He is our leader.

Be patient. God knows exactly what we need and when we need it.

Matthew 6:26 "Look at all the birds – do you think they worry about their existence? They don't plant or reap or store up food, yet your heavenly Father provides them each with food. Aren't you much more valuable to your Father than they?" (TPT) If we rush His timing, disaster could be just around the corner.

Can you think of a time where you rushed? Where you failed to pray, failed to wait and failed to be patient? Perhaps it was impatience on waiting for God's answer on that job proposal. Maybe you failed to consult with God on that marriage proposal before you said yes. Or were you impatient on that big move across the country. Hindsight is always 20/20, but if we will **be patient** and **wait for God's timing**, **He WILL** show us the way and it is for our own good.

I encourage you to go look up **Exodus 32**. It speaks of when Moses was on the mountain getting the Lord's commandments and the people became impatient waiting for Moses to come down, and so they pleaded with Aaron to erect an alter to which they could worship. When God saw this, He wasn't just mad, He was FURIOUS! He reprimanded Moses and commanded him to get down from the mountain and the Lord told Moses He was going to destroy the people, but Moses prayed for them and asked God not to destroy them all. God listened to Moses. However, many people did perish as they chose wrongly and did not stand with the Lord.

Be patient. Don't forget about your past victories and blessings like the Israelites did. They forgot all about God's miracles and provisions.

God will be there for you. **He will** show you the answer in His timing.

Psalms 46:10 "Be still, and know that I am God; I will be exalted among the nations, I will be exalted in the earth!" (NKJV)

I SCREWED UP

Since we talked about Aaron and Moses yesterday, let's continue a bit. Is there still hope when we screw up? The answer is, without a doubt, **there is hope**. This is called **forgiveness and grace**. God gives it so freely.

Aaron royally screwed up. He allowed the Israelites to talk him into something he knew was dreadfully wrong, yet he did it anyway. Guess what... God used him anyway. Aaron repented of his sins and God still placed him in great authority as a priest **(Exodus 32:2-5)**.

Moses killed a man before they left Egypt and God still used him to lead **ALL** the Israelites out of Egypt **(Exodus 2:12)**.

Adam and Eve disobeyed, yet God still loved them and even made them clothing before He banned them from Eden **(Genesis 3:6-24)**.

Jonah ran from God, but He still used him to deliver a message. **Jonah 1-3**

God wants to use you and doesn't care what, how or when you screwed up in the past. He knows you will screw up in the future. He **DOES** want you to repent when you sin or screw up.

So, **STOP** using your past to hinder your future. God knows. He may not be pleased, but He still loves you anyway. If you don't leave the past, in the past what good are you doing yourself or those around you? Listen to me...no matter what your past, perhaps it's infidelity, theft, murder, sexual indiscretions, lying, pride, coveting, God has seen, and He is willing to forgive if only you **come to Him** and **turn from your sin**. Now you can't keep on sinning! You should put a stop to it IMMEDI-ATELY! And if you screw up again after you have asked for forgiveness, you go back to the cross again and lay it down again and repent. God knows your heart.

God sent His son to die on the cross for your sins. If you haven't accepted that gift, isn't it high time you kneel down and open that package? Christ laid down his life for the sinner. That would be you. If you haven't accepted Jesus Christ as your Lord and Savior, please turn to Day 30 to see how simple it is to accept this gift.

Romans 3:23 "For all have sinned and fall short of the Glory of God." (NKJV)

John 3:16 "For God so loved the world that He gave His only begotten Son, that whoever believes in Him, should not perish but have everlasting life." (NKJV)

SUNGLASSES

I'm not sure the skin tone that God blessed you with, but I am so pale that I'm almost see-through. I was wearing shorts one day and one of my friends walks up snickering and says, "Wow! I need to wear sunglasses around you. Your legs are blinding me they are so white!" Y'all, they are super light and possibly a little reflective in the sun, but they are my God-given legs and flesh tone, so I'm okay with it.

As Christians, we should all have people putting on their sunglasses around us. Not, of course, because of our reflective legs, but because the Light of Jesus is shining so brightly through us.

Once we have accepted Christ, we throw off the old and clothe ourselves with the new. The new is filled with **Joy, Acceptance, Courage and Strength**. We get all this because Jesus had all of this and he freely gives it to us. He now lives within us and is called Light.

John 1:9 "For the Light of Truth was about to come into the world and shine upon everyone." (TPT)

John 8:12 "Then Jesus spoke to them again, saying, 'I am the light of the world. He who follows Me shall not walk in the darkness, but will have the light of life.'" (NKJV)

GIFT EXCHANGE

··

When Christmas comes around and you get invited to family parties or church parties, you often have gift exchanges. These gift exchanges are often fun, but truly the gift you get is not always what you would want. You probably bought a generic gift that might be a fit for any person. Even though we enjoy the fun, we don't receive everlasting joy from these gift exchanges.

Let me tell you a story about the greatest gift exchange in **ALL** of eternity. This gift exchange is open to all of mankind and open to you. Trust me, you don't want to miss out on this great gift, the greatest gift. The package is wrapped with exquisite, fine, and elegant paper tied with the most precious bow on top. It's almost so beautiful that you don't want to untie the bow or rip off the paper. But here is the deal, that is the **ONLY** way to get to the goodness inside. Your blessings that await inside are more precious than you could ever have imagined for yourself.

Are you ready for the BIG reveal?

God sent His son, Jesus Christ. This is YOUR GIFT. You must exchange your heart for eternal life. If you give Jesus your heart, He will give you eternal life with promises of everlasting joy. He will reside in you forever. If you were the only human on the face of this earth, He would do it all over again and die a torturous death, **JUST. FOR. YOU.** Exchange your soiled clothes of sin for His white rob of purity.

There is **NOTHING** you have done in the past that can stop you from receiving **HIS GIFT**. This special heartfelt gift that was picked out is just for you. It is personal and loving. God accepts you as you are right now. He doesn't care if you have broken all ten commandments or more, He still wants you to come into His everlasting embrace. He wants you to know Him, not in your head, but from your heart. Jesus wants a personal relationship with you. He wants to walk with you and talk with you for the rest of your Earth-filled days. Then He wants to spend eternity with you in His Father's house. Jesus is there, now, in Heaven, designing the most extraordinary home. HGTV ain't got nothing in the stunning layout, design, and love that is contained there.

John 14:2-4 "In My Father's house are many mansions; if it were not so, I would have told you. I go to prepare a place for you. And if I go and prepare a place for you, I will come again and receive you to Myself; that where I am, there you may be also. And where I go you know, and the way you know." (NKJV)

What are you waiting for? This gift is free. No strings attached. You don't deserve this gift, and He is giving it anyway. How precious is that? The only catch is... you have to receive it. You are the only one that has the power to unwrap it.

Please don't put this book down and think about it. Don't say, "maybe later I'll invite Jesus over for dinner". Tomorrow is NOT promised. Guess what, our next minute is NOT promised. If you feel your heart strings being pulled, that is Jesus calling to you. The most dreadful and painful event that could ever happen to you is to NOT accepting Christ as your Savior, then die and have eternal separation from your Heavenly Father.

Receiving this gift is as simple as saying,

"Lord I know you died for all my sins. Please forgive me all my sins. I know you are the Son of God. I want to have everlasting life through you. I accept you and want to follow you all the days of my life. Amen"

If you have just said this prayer and meant it with your whole heart... welcome to the family of Christ. You now have royal blood flowing through your veins. Please take a moment to read the following verses about salvation.

Romans 3:23 "For all have sinned, and fall short of the glory of God." (NKJV)

1 John 4:9-10 "The light of God's love shined within us when he sent his matchless Son into the world so that we might live through him. This is love: He loved us long before we loved him. It was his love, not ours. He proved it by sending his Son to be the pleasing sacrificial offering to take away our sins." (TPT)

Matthew 11:28 "Come to Me all you who labor and are heavy laden, and I will give your rest." (NKJV)

Romans 5:8 "But God demonstrates His own love toward us, in that, while we were still sinners, Christ died for us." (NKJV)

John 1:12 "But as many as received Him, to them He gave the right to become children of God, to those who believe in His name." (NKJV)

Romans 10:9 "That if you confess with your mouth the Lord Jesus and believe in your heart that God has raised Him from the dead, you will be saved." (NKJV)

Now that you have accepted this gift and choose to follow Jesus, I just want to say, it will not be easy. Jesus did not promise smooth sailing all the days of our lives.

John 16:33 "These things I have spoken to you, that in Me you may have peace. In the world you will have tribulation; but be of good cheer, I have overcome the world." (NKJV) He does promise we live in a sinful world and He will never forsake us.

Psalms 94:14 "For the Lord will never walk away from the cherished ones, nor would he forsake his chosen ones who belong to him." (TPT)

The enemy is out to kill, steal and destroy, so especially now in your infant stage of Christian growth, He will try to trip you up, throw in roadblocks along the way. Satan will try to convince you that you still aren't good enough. He will try to bring up ALL your past sins. Plug your ears; turn up the volume of God's word; and lay it down at the cross! I will not lie to you; you may have to lay it at the cross over and over again. I know there have been many things in my past that the enemy still haunts me with, and as soon as I am on to his trick, I take it swiftly to Jesus' feet and ask Him to take it back. He already took it, but we sometimes like to go get it back from Him. Don't do that!

Now there is some action that I highly encourage you to do as a new believer or perhaps you just rededicated yourself to the Lord. Get in The Word. Also, find a great church home.

This is where you can get connected with other believers. I also suggest getting an accountability partner. As humans we typically seem to be more on task and grow when we have someone we can enlist to hold us accountable for our actions.

I'm so happy for your courage in accepting a gift that is filled with so much. I love you and pray that God shines His light through you and to you.

LET'S GROW, GLOW & GO!!!!

....

What area of your life have you capped your capabilities?

_____

_____

_____

Satan, aka, liar, murderer, enemy, deceiver, and guilt provoker is out to destroy us! He wants us to superglue a lid on our accomplishments, our dreams and our abilities. Liar does not want us to **grow, glow or go**. He wants to poison our roots, extinguish our flame and stop our engine.

Only the Light, Truth, The ALPHA and OMEGA, Prince of Peace and our Savior can annihilate the enemy's advances. Jesus is the

One that will fertilize and water, ignite His light in us, and rev us up to progress.

Short story:

My 3-1/2 pound Chihuahua that we brought home at six weeks old and would only fit in the palm of our hand. Because of his size I would always pick him up and put him on our couch and bed. Well... to this day, six years later, he doesn't even attempt to jump on our bed or couch. Is it because he can't? NO, it's because his capabilities have been capped and he doesn't envision the process or the success. This realization only came to me after we got another 3-1/2 pound Chihuahua three years ago. Princess can jump up on the couch without hesitation. However, I started lifting her up on our recliner which I had seen her jump up on many times before and when I began picking her up, she quit trying to do it by herself. When I realized I was stunting her growth and enabling her thoughts to think she couldn't jump, I quit picking her up. Eventually, she realized she could jump high enough again and I don't limit her capabilities any longer. Her potential is no longer capped.

God's design is not to stunt us, but to bloom us! Today I want you to take just a few short moments and dwell on the lies the enemy is whispering in your ear. Write them down.

Then take a few short moments and really listen to His spirit and see where God wants you to **grow**.

What enemy lies are you hearing?

_____

_____

_____

What <u>ARE</u> God's Truths?

_____

_____

_____

Are you having troubles? Don't worry. When I began my purposeful journey of growth in late 2017, it took me months to even begin to deprogram my thoughts and the lies that were in the atmosphere around me. If you are stumped, please **pray** and think of this throughout the day and then come back this evening and jot down just even a word or two. Don't let the Devil keep you from GOING into a GROWTH pattern that will keep you from

GLOWING! Please reflect on the below Bible passages to enhance your **growth** today.

Proverbs 29:18 "When there is no clear prophetic vision, people quickly wander astray. But when you follow the revelation of the word, heaven's bliss fills your soul." (TPT)

Matthew 19:26 "Jesus looked at them and said, 'With man this is impossible, but with God all things are possible.' " (NIV)

Liar and Murderer - Look up **John 8:44**

Enemy - Look up **Matthew 13:39**

The End

ADVENTURE AWAITS YOU

....

Thank you for reading this 31-day devotional. I pray that it spoke to you every day. I hope this inspired you to spend more time with God daily and from this day forward. I hope it gave you courage to go after your God-given goals and dreams.

Life with Jesus is such a fabulous adventure! Be sure to pack the right supplies in your suitcase and drop the baggage at the cross before and during your journey. I pray that you embrace it moment-by-moment. Don't be discouraged by the season of life you are in right now. Just breathe, then repeat and breathe again.

I believe in you and I'm cheering you on. Even more importantly, Jesus is your biggest fan and He has His eyes on you every step of the way. You can do this. One. Breath. At. A. Time.

Colossians 2:6 "So then, just as you received Christ Jesus as Lord, continue to live your lives in him, strengthened in the faith as you were taught, and overflowing with thankfulness." (NIV)

—

About the Author

DeEsta Dawn was born and raised in East Texas and grew up in the quaint town of Canton, and is still a Texas resident today.

Her life's pupose is the pursuit of God even when she falls short in life's daily tasks. DeEsta is a proud mother of two children from her first marriage. When she remarried seven years ago to Stevan, she was blessed with three "I-do" children. She owns a 20 year old company which sets up businesses with merchant credit card accounts. In her free time, DeEsta enjoys being with family and friends as much as possible. She also loves the peacefulness of sitting outside their country home and watching God's great artwork in action.

To find out more about DeEsta, please visit her website at DeEstaDawn.com or send an email at DeEstaDawn@gmail.com.

You can also explore her devotional videos on You Tube: *Tea Fiesta with DeEsta*.

Made in the USA
Coppell, TX
14 November 2019

11353750R00066